The Thirty-Six Stratagems for Young Minds

The Siege Strategy

Edited by **KaDa Gushi** and **Hongyan Mao**
Illustrated by **Chen Wei Studio**

Books Beyond Boundaries
ROYAL COLLINS

Long ago, during the Warring States period, there was a legendary strategist named Guiguzi. Among his many students, two stood out: Pang Juan and Sun Bin.

Both were brilliant, but Pang Juan was jealous of Sun Bin's intelligence.

After finishing his studies, Pang Juan became a powerful general in the State of Wei. Fearing that Sun Bin would outshine him, he tricked his old friend, leading to Sun Bin's cruel punishment—his legs were crippled. However, Sun Bin escaped to the State of Qi, where he became a trusted military advisor.

In BC 354, General Pang Juan led a large Wei army to attack the State of Zhao, aiming to seize its capital, Handan. Wei's forces surrounded the city, cutting off supplies and launching powerful assaults.

"Disaster! The enemy has burned our grain stores!" a Zhao soldier cried.

"Look out!" another shouted as a massive boulder crashed into the city walls, leaving a gaping hole.

Pang Juan was a master of warfare. He ordered his soldiers to burn Zhao's food supplies and used powerful siege weapons—catapults (投石车)—to bombard the city.

The situation grew dire. The King of Zhao had no choice but to send an urgent plea to the State of Qi:

"Handan is under siege! We need reinforcements at once!"

If Zhao fell, Qi would be next. The King of Qi called his generals for counsel, seeking a way to stop Wei's advance.

The King of Qi wanted to appoint Sun Bin as the commander, but Sun Bin looked down at his crippled legs and sighed.

"I cannot march with the soldiers into battle," he said, "so I cannot be the general. But I can advise the commander and help defeat the Wei army."

Thus, the king appointed General Tian Ji as commander, and Sun Bin accompanied the army as its chief strategist. Together, they set out to aid the State of Zhao.

At first, Tian Ji planned to march directly to Handan, engage the Wei forces, and drive them away.

But Sun Bin shook his head repeatedly. "A tangled thread cannot be pulled apart by force. If two people are fighting, stepping between them and swinging wildly will only make things worse. We must find the enemy's weakness and force them to retreat on their own."

Tian Ji frowned. "But Handan is on the verge of falling! How can we make Wei withdraw?"

Sun Bin calmly explained, “Pang Juan has taken most of his elite troops to attack Zhao, leaving Wei’s capital, Daliang, poorly defended. If we strike Daliang instead of Handan, the King of Wei will have no choice but to order Pang Juan to return and defend his homeland.”

Tian Ji immediately recognized the brilliance of this plan. "Understood! We will march to Daliang and force them to abandon Handan!"

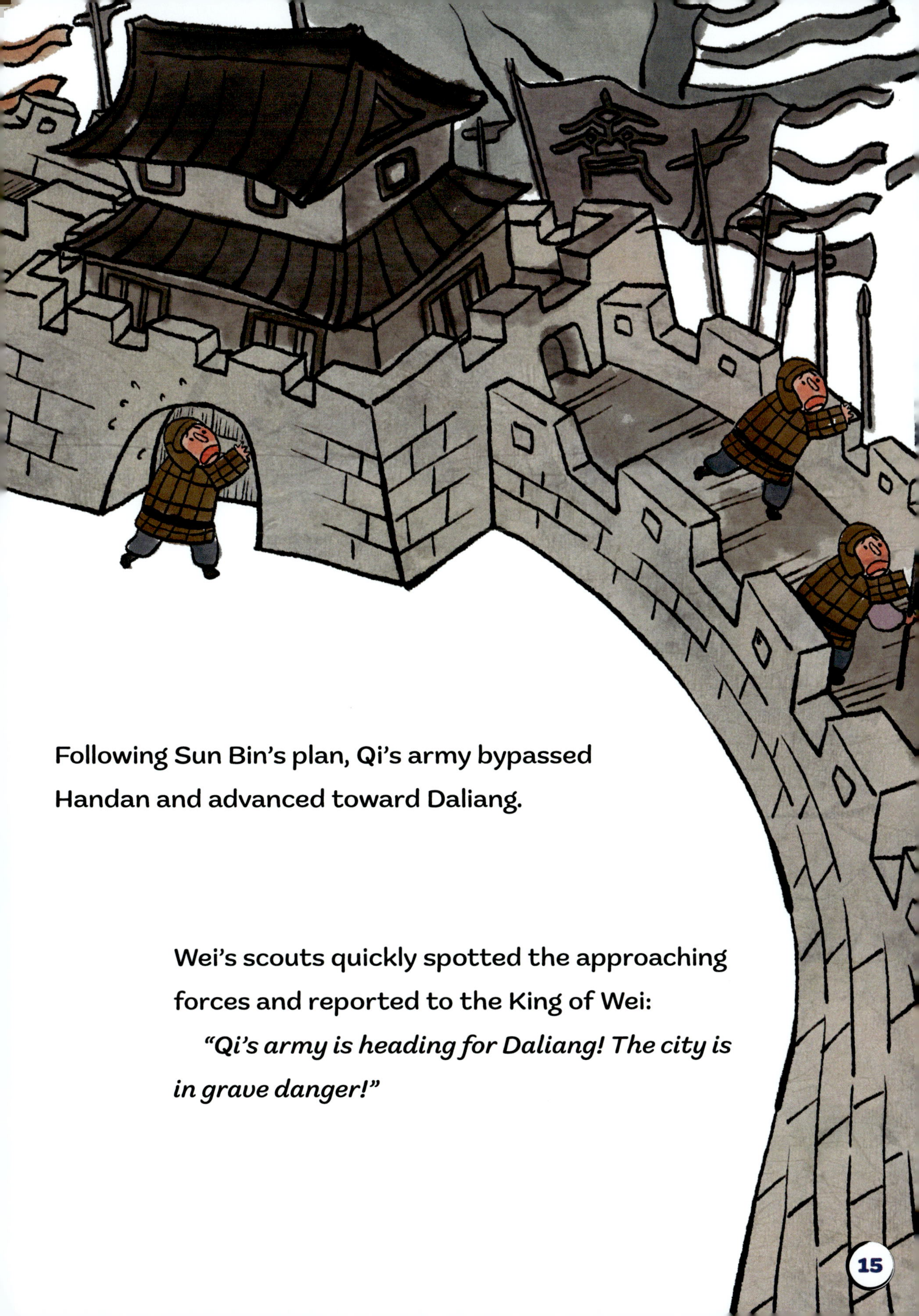

Following Sun Bin's plan, Qi's army bypassed Handan and advanced toward Daliang.

Wei's scouts quickly spotted the approaching forces and reported to the King of Wei:

"Qi's army is heading for Daliang! The city is in grave danger!"

加急

The King of Wei panicked. His capital was the heart of his kingdom—it could not be lost! He immediately dispatched urgent orders to Pang Juan:

“Return at once! Defend Daliang at all costs!”

Pang Juan and his troops had been fighting relentlessly for weeks. Exhausted and caught off guard by Qi’s unexpected maneuver, they had no choice but to abandon their siege of Handan and rush back toward Wei.

Little did they know—Sun Bin was waiting for them.

As Wei's army hurried home without rest, Qi's forces prepared an ambush near Guiling. The moment Pang Juan's soldiers arrived, Qi's rested troops launched a ferocious attack from all sides.

The battle was a disaster for Wei. Pang Juan barely escaped with a handful of soldiers, while Qi's forces claimed victory.

With his army shattered, Pang Juan had no choice but to withdraw completely from Zhao, saving Handan.

Huh!
韓

Years later, in BC 341, Wei once again waged war, this time attacking the State of Han.

Just like Zhao before, Han's ruler sent an urgent request to Qi for help. The King of Qi once again dispatched General Tian Ji and Sun Bin to rescue Han.

As they marched, Tian Ji turned to Sun Bin and asked, “Master Sun, how should we deal with Pang Juan this time?”

Sun Bin smiled knowingly. “The Wei army has always underestimated Qi, and Pang Juan is arrogant and proud. We will use the same ‘Besiege Wei to Rescue Zhao’ strategy again—what do you think?”

Tian Ji clapped his hands. “Brilliant! We shall attack Wei first and deal with Pang Juan when he returns!”

Just as before, Qi's army bypassed the main battlefield and attacked Daliang. When the King of Wei received word that Qi threatened the capital, he had to order Pang Juan to return immediately.

A messenger arrived at Pang Juan's camp with urgent orders: "General Pang! The Qi army is attacking Daliang! His Majesty commands you to return at once!"

Pang Juan immediately recognized the trick—Sun Bin had used this strategy before! But he had no choice. Disobeying the King of Wei's orders was not an option.

Frustrated but obedient, Pang Juan led his army back toward Wei.

魏

As soon as Pang Juan crossed into Wei's territory, another message arrived: "The Qi army has already withdrawn to their homeland!"

Pang Juan was furious. "It's that Sun Bin again! He tricked me again!" He clenched his fists and shouted, "Chase them down! Don't let them escape!"

However, this chase led Pang Juan straight into his doom. Sun Bin, knowing Pang Juan's arrogance, had carefully set a deadly ambush along the route, waiting for the perfect moment to strike.

For the third time, Pang Juan fell into Sun Bin's trap—but this time, there was no escape. His arrogance had sealed his fate.

The Legacy of "Besiege Wei to Rescue Zhao"

By attacking the enemy's weakness instead of confronting them head-on, Sun Bin outsmarted Pang Juan twice. His strategy became known as "Besiege Wei to Rescue Zhao," a brilliant example of how clever thinking can turn the tide of war.

Historical Notes

Guiguzi

A legendary strategist and teacher. His students, including Sun Bin and Pang Juan, played major roles in the battles of the Warring States period.

Pang Juan

A famous general of Wei, skilled in warfare but blinded by jealousy. His rivalry with Sun Bin led to his downfall.

Sun Bin

Once betrayed and crippled, he rose to become Qi's greatest strategist. Using his intelligence, he defeated Pang Juan twice and secured Qi's dominance.

Moral of the Story

True victory doesn't go to the strongest but to the one who thinks ahead!

Tian Ji

A general of Qi and a loyal follower of Sun Bin. He led Qi's forces in both victories against Wei.

Siege Weapons

Ancient armies used catapults (投石车) to hurl stones at city walls, breaking defenses and terrifying enemies.

Bamboo Scrolls

Before paper was invented, Chinese writing was recorded on bamboo strips tied together with string and rolled into scrolls.

About the Editor

Mao Hongyan is the associate editor of *Happy Chinese Language and Composition*, a children's magazine. With a deep passion for children's literature, she is highly dedicated to children's growth and has extensive experience in children's book planning. She understands child psychology and cognitive development, crafting texts that align with young readers' psychological characteristics. Her works are beloved by children and parents alike. She has published *Interactive Sound Book: Fun with Chinese Idioms*, produced by Lelequ.

About the Illustrator

Chen Wei, born in 1979 in Taizhou, Jiangsu, graduated from the Design Department of Xi'an Academy of Fine Arts.

His notable picture books include *A New Resident in Kano Town*, *The Mice of Rose Villa*, and *The Frog and the Boy*. Among them, *The Frog and the Boy* won the Second Feng Zikai Children's Picture Book Award Jury Prize. His works have been translated and published in Taiwan, Hong Kong, and South Korea.

The Thirty-Six Stratagems for Young Minds: The Siege Strategy

Edited by KaDa Gushi and Hongyan Mao
Illustrated by Chen Wei Studio

First published in 2025 by Royal Collins Publishing Group Inc.
Groupe Publication Royal Collins Inc.
550-555 boul. René-Lévesque O Montréal (Québec) H2Z1B1 Canada

ISBN: 978-1-4878-1337-6

To find out more about our publications,
please visit www.royalcollins.com.